Tolley's
National Insurance
Contributions
2008

Pre-Budget Report Supplement

Edited by Jon Golding ATT TEP

Consulting Editor Peter Arrowsmith FCA

D0755640

Members of the LexisNexis Group worldwide

United Kingdom	LexisNexis, a Division of Reed Elsevier (UK) Ltd, Halsbury House, 35 Chancery Lane, London, WC2A 1EL, and London House, 20-22 East London Street, Edinburgh EH7 4BQ
Argentina	LexisNexis Argentina, Buenos Aires
Australia	LexisNexis Butterworths, Chatswood, New South Wales
Austria	LexisNexis Verlag ARD Orac GmbH & Co KG, Vienna
Benelux	LexisNexis Benelux, Amsterdam
Canada	LexisNexis Canada, Markham, Ontario
Chile	LexisNexis Chile Ltda, Santiago
China	LexisNexis China, Beijing and Shanghai
France	LexisNexis SA, Paris
Germany	LexisNexis Deutschland GmbH, Munster
Hong Kong	LexisNexis Hong Kong, Hong Kong
India	LexisNexis India, New Delhi
Italy	Giuffrè Editore, Milan
Japan	LexisNexis Japan, Tokyo
Malaysia	Malayan Law Journal Sdn Bhd, Kuala Lumpur
Mexico	LexisNexis Mexico, Mexico
New Zealand	LexisNexis NZ Ltd, Wellington
Poland	Wydawnictwo Prawnicze LexisNexis Sp, Warsaw
Singapore	LexisNexis Singapore, Singapore
South Africa	LexisNexis Butterworths, Durban
USA	LexisNexis, Dayton, Ohio

© Reed Elsevier (UK) Ltd 2008

Published by LexisNexis

A CIP Catalogue record for this book is available from the British Library.

ISBN 9780754534648

Printed and bound in Great Britain by Hobbs the Printers Ltd, Hampshire

Visit LexisNexis at www.lexisnexis.co.uk

About This Pre-Budget Report Statement Supplement

This Pre-Budget Report supplement to the 2008–09 book gives details of changes in the law and practice in connection with National Insurance contributions from the publication of Tolley's National Insurance Contributions 2008–09 up until the Pre-Budget Report Statement on 24 November 2008. It lists the changes in the same order and under the same paragraph headings as the annual publication but will where necessary for completeness be shown next to the original text.

Each time Tolley's National Insurance Contributions 2008–09 is used, reference should be made to the material contained in this supplement. The Contents gives a list of all the chapters and paragraphs which have been updated.

Her Majesty's Revenue & Customs (HMRC) texts are Crown copyright and are produced by kind permission of the Controller of Her Majesty's Stationery Office.

Former Contributions Agency and HMRC texts are Crown copyright and reproduced by kind permission of the Agency, HMRC and the Controller of Her Majesty's Stationery Office.

Tax Bulletin and National Insurance News contains certain qualifications that appear in each issue. These should be referred to before reliance is placed on an interpretation.

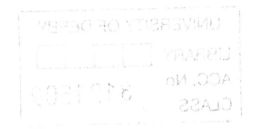

Contents

This supplement contains amendments to the chapters and paragraphs of Tolley's National Insurance Contributions 2008–09 as listed below.

Contents

2 Administration

Replace the first half of the Table on page 12 in 2.1 with the following:

Longbenton, Newcastle upon Tyne, NE98 1ZZ

Deferment Group	Deferment of Class 1, 2 and 4 contributions	Tel 08459 157141
Self Employment Services	Class 2 and Class 3 (including direct debit)	Tel 08459 154655
		Fax 08459 153417
Newly Self Employed Helpline	Advises newly self employed persons on general Inland Revenue matters and accepts Class 2 registrations by phone	Tel 08459 154515
Overseas Conts Helpline		Tel 08459 154811 (from overseas – 44 191 203 7010)
		Fax 08459 157800 (from overseas – 44 191 225 7800)
Overseas Conts – general (from UK)		Tel 0191 225 4811
Overseas Conts – general (from abroad)		Tel 44 191 203 7010
Overseas Conts (EC)	NI for persons moving in EC/EEA	Tel 0191 225 3886
Overseas Conts (RA)	NI for persons moving outside EC/EEA	Tel 0191 225 3299
Refunds Group	Refunds on NI paid in error or excess	Tel 08459 159464
NISPI	All aspects of contracted-out employment	Tel 08459 150150
Posting Check Group	Computer check problems re reduced rate elections, age exception etc.	Tel 08459 154553
Age exception	Applications for certificates	Tel 08456 060265
General enquiries from individuals		Tel 08453 021479

8 Anti-Avoidance

Insert the following paragraph at the end of 8.5 on page 89:

The *National Insurance Contributions (Application of Part 7 of the Finance Act 2004) (Amendment) Regulations 2008, SI 2008/2678* made further changes in line with those made to the scheme disclosure rules made by *Finance Act 2007* and *Finance Act 2008*. The *Finance Act 2007* powers for the Commissioners of HM Revenue and Customs to require by notice scheme promoters to explain why a scheme is not notifiable; apply to the Special Commissioners for orders to provide information; or for orders that a scheme is or is not notifiable all extend to NIC from 1 November 2008. The *Finance Act 2008* changes in regard to 'Scheme Reference Numbers' (SRNs) also extend to NIC from 1 November 2008 – the co-promoter rule having been amended to ensure that all promoters receive a SRN, that they are required to pass them to clients and that clients are required to pass those SRNs to other users of the scheme in question. In appropriate circumstances form AAG6 will be used.

9   Appeals and Reviews

Replace the last two sentences in 9.8 on page 106 with the following:

Spectrum Computer Supplies Ltd v HMRC [2006] STC SCD 668 Sp C 559 (**8.1** ANTI-AVOIDANCE) and also *PA Holdings Ltd v HMRC* [2008] STC SCD 1185 Sp C 707 where a joint PAYE and NICs hearing did not prejudice the taxpayer company. See also **31** EARNINGS FROM EMPLOYMENT: READILY CONVERTIBLE ASSETS, ETC.

Replace section 9.17 on page 117 with the following:

9.17   The future of NIC appeals

A consultation white paper issued in July 2004 (Cm 6243), 'Transforming Public Services: Complaints Redress and Tribunals' (CP 07/05), proposed a unified tax jurisdiction under a new tribunal system having two-tiers. The first tier will hear virtually all first instance direct and indirect tax appeals. This will include NICs appeals. Appeals against these first tier decisions will go to an appellate tier where permission has been granted or on a point of law. *The Tribunals, Courts and Enforcement Act 2007* will introduce these changes from, it is expected, April 2009. However, changes to appeals in respect of social security matters (which will include Home Responsibilities Protection and contracting out matters) are likely to be made in late 2008.See Treasury Press Release, 3 November 2008.

In preparation for the new systems, *FA 2008, s 124* authorises a scheme whereby decisions (including NIC decisions) may be subject to internal review before proceeding to formal appeal. This is being trialled (at the option of the 'customer') during 2008.

The new system will be headed by Lord Justice Carnworth as Senior President and have its own judiciary, Rules of Procedure and a new location for processing direct tax appeals. It will be independent of HM Revenue and Customs, who currently control listing and other aspects of case management in the General Commissioners system, which many outside observers have always doubted was sufficiently distanced from HM Revenue and Customs. This new Central Processing Centre (CPC) for direct tax appeals will be located in Birmingham in the new Tribunals Service Pathfinder Administrative Support Centre, where specialist tax/NIC appeals work will be dealt with by dedicated tax appeals staff. There will be a network of 130 hearing centres across the country and the facility for additional private hirings.

The Tribunals Service has been working in partnership with the Judicial Appointments Commission to recruit 18 legal Members (four of whom will be full time) and 75 non-legal Member positions. These posts will be filled early in 2009, so that Members can be trained fully in time for the planned April 2009 start.

It is expected that the main differences that users will see will be that appeal notices will be sent directly to the Tribunals Service by the appellant rather than to HM Revenue and Customs, there will be four procedural tracks depending on the complexity of the appeal and there will be a new costs regime.

Members of the judiciary will work at the CPC in order to give judicial direction where required and manage cases appropriately. There will also be two full-time, tax-dedicated registrars at the CPC, who will carry out quasi-judicial functions, eg categorise cases received at the CPC into tracks, identify tax cases which are complex (and therefore eligible to enter the costs regime) and bring these to the attention of the judiciary for a decision; liaise with the Upper Tribunal regarding those rare cases which start at that court, or which appeal to it from the First-tier.

The route of appeal from the First-tier will be to the Upper Tribunal, which is a superior court of record akin to the High Court. Appeal to the Upper Tribunal will be on a point of law only, and with permission of the First-tier or the Upper Tribunal. The exception to this will be those extremely rare cases which start in the Upper Tribunal, where onward appeals will be to the Court of Appeal or the Court of Sessions in Scotland.

11   Armed Forces

Replace point (g) in 11.3 on pages 126 and 127 with the following:

(g)   with effect from 1 April 2008, Council Tax Relief payments designated by the Secretary of State for Defence to members of the armed forces. This is an operational welfare package that will give relief on 25% of council tax whilst Forces personnel are on operations. [*Social Security (Contributions) Regulations 2001, SI 2001/1004, Sch 3 Part VIII para 12B,* inserted by *Social Security (Contributions) (Amendment No 2) Regulations 2008, SI 2008/607, Reg 3; ITEPA 2003, s 297B,* inserted by *FA 2008, s 51*].

See HM Revenue and Customs National Insurance Manual NIM32006.

12   Arrears of Contributions

Replace the last paragraph in 12.1 on pages 131 and 132 with the following:

Following consultation in 2007 and 2008, steps have been taken to harmonise collection of the various duties for which HM Revenue and Customs is responsible (including National Insurance contributions) as well as providing means to set an overpayment of one duty against an underpayment of another. *FA 2008, s 127* (taking control of goods), *s 130* (set-off).

Replace the last paragraph of 12.6 on page 137 and the first paragraph on page 138 with the following:

Although *s 9(1)* prevents an action to recover any sum recoverable by virtue of any enactment from being brought after the expiration of six years from the date on which the cause of action accrued, *s 29(5)* of that Act treats the cause of action as having accrued on the date that any person liable for a debt, or his authorised agent, acknowledges it in a signed document or makes any payment in respect of it. Acknowledgement of a smaller sum than that demanded is an acknowledgement only of that smaller sum (*Surrendra Overseas Ltd v Government of Sri Lanka* [1977] 2 AER 481), whereas a general admission of debt will be regarded as an acknowledgement of the whole of the debt if the precise amount can be ascertained by extrinsic evidence (*Dungate v Dungate* [1965] 3 AER 818). Acknowledgement of the debt can be made electronically. In the Court of Appeal case, *Good Challenger Navegante SA v Metalexportimport SA* [2003] 1 Lloyds Report 471 a telex with typed signature was sent and was held to comply with the requirements of *Limitation Act 1980*. It was intended as a signature and the court said that it must look to the function and not its form. An electronic signature is 'anything in electronic form that is incorporated into or otherwise logically associated with any electronic communication or electronic data' [*Electronic Communications Act 2000, section 7*]. The *Limitation Act 1980* does not apply in Scotland where equivalent legislation provides instead a five year time limit. [*Prescription and Limitation (Scotland) Act 1973, s 6(1)*].

13 Benefits: Contributions Requirements

Replace the last paragraph of 12.11 on page 144 with the following:

From Royal Assent to the *Finance Act 2008*, HM Revenue and Customs will have the power to act on its own volition to set an overpayment of one duty for which it is responsible against an underpayment of another. Previously, this could happen only at the request of, or with the consent of, the individual or body concerned. [*ITA 2007, s 429; FA 2008, s 130.*]

13 Benefits: Contributions Requirements

Add the following paragraph to the end of 13.4 on page 155:

More recently in *Carson and Others v United Kingdom* ECR, [2008] TLR 20 November 2008 (Application No 42184/05) the exclusion of certain pensioners living abroad from the index-linked uprating scheme applicable to all pensioners in the UK was not in breach of *Human Rights Act 1998, Art 14*. The EHCR agreed with the British Government that it did not exceed its very broad discretion on matters of macro economic policy by entering into different reciprocal agreements with certain countries and not others. In addition, the British Government had taken steps to, in a series of leaflets, which referred to the implications of moving abroad and the absence of index linking for pensions in certain countries. [*Social Security Benefits Up-rating Order 2001, SI 2001/910*]. See also **43.2** LEAFLETS AND FORMS and **51** OVERSEAS MATTERS.

14 Categorisation

Replace point (b) in 14.13 on page 173 with the following:

(*b*) Erroneously paid Class 2 contributions *may* be reallocated as primary Class 1 contributions, but no legal obligation to reallocate is imposed on the Department. The matter is within the discretion of HM Revenue and Customs. [*Social Security (Contributions) Regulations 2001, SI 2001/1004, Reg 51*]. In addition, following the merger in 1999 with the then Inland Revenue, it has increasingly been the practice to give credit for Class 4 also – though such credit is by no means automatic. See HM Revenue and Customs Employer Compliance Handbook ECH11060.

Insert following sentences in place of the existing ones at the foot of page 174 in 14.13:

Even assuming HM Revenue and Customs permits the set-off of Class 2 contributions and Class 4 contributions already paid by A, it may request an amount due from B (but see **12.6** ARREARS OF CONTRIBUTIONS as regards its enforceability) of £63,285.33 (ie £88,186.75 – £2,467.75 – £22,433.67) and *only a small part of this amount relating to 2007-08 may be recoverable from A*. If, however, A had misled B the position might alter. See **21.7** COLLECTION.

Replace the first sentence in the second paragraph on page 176 in 14.13 with the following:

The effect of this is that Bloggs TV Rentals Ltd should pay only £34,780.81 (£88,186.75 *less* the total Class 1 liabilities (as reduced by Class 2 and Class 4 paid) for the years ended 5 April 1996, 5 April 1997, 5 April 1998, 5 April 1999, 5 April 2000, 5 April 2001 and 5 April 2002).

Replace the last two sentences in the second paragraph of 14.13 on page 177 with the following:

In notes published by HM Revenue and Customs, no action is proposed on National Insurance but the wording makes clear that – now that the department deals with both income tax and National Insurance – HM Revenue and Customs is often in a position to set off the recategorised employee's Class 4 liability against the Class 1 liability (see www.hmrc.gov.uk/

employers/faq-transfer-paye.htm and HM Revenue and Customs Employer Compliance Handbook ECH11060). This is an obvious improvement on the 1984 Hansard statement quoted earlier and affected businesses should therefore press for complete set-off of both Class 2 contributions and Class 4 contributions in all cases.

16   Class 1A Contributions: Benefits in Kind

Replace the existing statutory reference in the last sentence of the third paragraph in 16.5 on page 218:

[*ITEPA 2003, s 139* as amended by *FA 2008, s 47*].

Insert the following paragraph at the end of the section 16.18 on page 232:

Nonetheless, this can still lead to slightly different applications in procedures from one area of the country to another. Therefore, HM Revenue and Customs is to introduce a standard method of calculation for the trade with effect from 6 April 2009. Details will be at Employment Income Manual EIM23650 to EIM23667 in due course but can in the meantime be accessed at http://www.hmrc.gov.uk/cars/averaging.pdf.

Replace the existing statutory reference in the last sentence of the first paragraph in 16.19 on page 233:

[*ITEPA 2003, s 160; Social Security (Contributions) Regulations 2001, SI 2001/1004, Sch 3* as amended by *Social Security (Contributions)(Amendment No 2) Regulations 2008, SI 2008/607, Reg 3; FA 2008, s 48*].

Replace the existing paragraph 16.28 on page 237 with the following:

16.28   Holiday homes abroad

A very welcome change announced in the 2007 Budget was that directors will no longer face a benefit in kind charge (many may not have realised that technically they did) where they own a home abroad (not in the UK) through the medium of a company. The new tax legislation excludes from tax liability any situation where the property is owned by a company owned by individuals, the company's only activities are ones that are incidental to its ownership of the property (eg letting when not in use by the owner and/or family members), the property is the company's only or main asset and the property is not funded directly or indirectly by a connected company. [*ITEPA 2003, ss 100A, 100B* as inserted by *FA 2008, s 45*]. HM Revenue and Customs said that it would not seek tax prior to the legislation taking effect and this is confirmed in *Finance Act 2008, s 45(2)*. Due to the structure of the Class 1A system the change in tax legislation will flow through automatically for Class 1A purposes.

The exemption has been extended from that in the draft legislation issued in summer 2007 to include cases where the company that owns the property is in turn owned by a holding company which does no more than own the shares in its subsidiary. The definition of the latter is as in *ITA 2007, s 992* being any body corporate or an unincorporated association other than a partnership, a local authority or a local authority association. It is therefore sufficiently wide to include bodies such as a Societe Civile Immobilliere (SCI) in France and a Limited Liability Company (LLC) in the USA. In addition, the exemption will not be prejudiced where the property is rented out to third parties when not being used by members and friends of the family.

The provisions are considered by HM Revenue and Customs to include time-shares.

The tax and related Class 1A charges will still apply where the property was acquired from a connected company at undervalue, a connected company directly or indirectly incurs expenditure on the property or directly or indirectly lends money after the property is acquired, or the accommodation is provided in pursuance of an arrangement the main purpose (or one of the main purposes) of which is the avoidance of tax or National Insurance.

21 Collection

It is believed that no-one has been required to actually pay Class 1A (or income tax) in respect of such 'benefits' previously, though arguably the law – certainly following *R v Dimsey* and *R v Allen* (74 TC 263) – was in fact unequivocal.

Indeed, there may still be an issue in some cases. Due to the nature of the law of property in certain countries the ownership of the holiday home may be through a trust, or the shares in the company owning the property may be held in one or more trusts. No relief is offered in these situations and whilst the past inactivity was welcome it must be assumed that from now on HM Revenue and Customs officers will enforce liability that falls outside the *FA 2008* parameters.

See HM Revenue and Customs Employment Income Manual EIM11371-11374.

21 Collection

Replace the last sentence in the first paragraph on page 265 in 21.3:

Clearly, from 2008–09 onwards the 'combined' payslips make identification of payment more difficult, but if in really exceptional circumstances such identification was required a letter enclosing a cheque and making the sender's requirements clear would be necessary or alternatively, if paying electronically, two separate monthly payments could be made denoting each with the appropriate prefix at the start of the collection reference number, viz 'N' (NICs) or 'P' (PAYE tax), for example for PAYE payments, P123PA00012345 and for National Insurance contributions, N123PA00012345.

22 Company Directors

Insert the following sentence at the end of the chapter on page 325 in paragraph 22.10:

See also *HMRC v Holland & Holland (re Paycheck Services 3 Ltd and other companies)* Ch D [2008] All ER (D) 319.

24 Credits

Replace the first two paragraphs in 24.2 on page 336 with the following:

(*d*) in the case of a credit of earnings for a year, such amount as is needed to bring the person's earnings factor (see EARNINGS FACTORS (**28**)) to the level at which the second contribution condition for entitlement to benefit will be satisfied for that year (see **13.2** BENEFITS).

[*Credits Regs, Reg 3(2)*, as amended by *Credits Amendment Regs 1987, Reg 3(c)* for 1987–88 and subsequent years and *Reg 11* for 1986–87 and earlier years].

Replace the points (i) to (iii) and the following statutory reference on page 339 in 24.8:

A disabled person is entitled to credits for a Government funded course which

(i) lasts 15 hours a week or more, and

(ii) lasts for longer than a year, or

(iii) is a Guide-Dog for the Blind training course.

[*Credits Regs, Reg 7* as amended by *Credits Amendment (No 3) Regs 1988, SI 1988/1545,*

Reg 2, Reg 2 from 4 September 1988 and *Enterprise (Scotland) Consequential Amendments Order 1991, Art 3(a)*].

Replace the points (c) and (d) at the end of 24.9 on page 341 with the following:

(c)   the year other than that for which credits are sought must be a year for which the EARNINGS FACTOR **(28)** is not less than 50 times that year's Lower Earnings Limit (see **33** EARNINGS LIMITS AND THRESHOLDS); and

(d)   the year for which credits are sought must not be a year before the person attains the age of 18.

The credits are, however, conditional upon the course or the apprenticeship having commenced before the person attained the age of 21 and having terminated.

[*Credits Regs, Reg 8* as amended by *Credits Amendment Regs 1989, Reg 3, Enterprise (Scotland) Consequential Amendments Order 1991, Art 3(b), Incapacity Benefit Consequential Transitional Amendments and Savings Regs 1995, Reg 6* and *Social Security (Credits and Contributions) (Jobseeker's Allowance Consequential and Miscellaneous Amendments) Regulations 1996, SI 1996/2367, Reg 2(5)*].

Replace the statutory reference in the second paragraph on page 342 in 24.10 with the following:

[*Credits Regs 8A, 8B,* inserted by *Social Security (Credits and Contributions)(Jobseeker's Allowance Consequential and Miscellaneous Amendments) Regs 1996, SI 1996/2367, Reg 2* as amended by *Social Security (Credits) Amendment Regs 2003, SI 2003/521, Reg 2* and *The Social Security (Miscellaneous Amendments) (No 3) Regulations 2007, SI 2007/1749, Reg 8.* Prior to 7 October 1996, *Credits Regs, Reg 9(1)(6)(9),* as amended by *Credits Amendment Regs 1977, Reg 2; Credits Amendment Regs 1978, Reg 2(2); Credits Amendment Regs 1983, Reg 2; Credits Amendment Regs 1987, Reg 11* for 1986–87 and earlier years, *Credits Amendment No 2 Regs 1987, Reg 2,* and *Credits Amendment No 4 Regs 1988, Reg 2(3)(b),* for 1987–88 to 6 October 1996, and *Credits Amendment Regs 1988, Regs 2 and 3* for 1988–1989 to 6 October 1996 and *Incapacity Benefit Consequential and Transitional Amendments and Savings Regs 1995, Reg 6*].

Replace the first two paragraphs of 24.14 on page 344 with the following:

For the purpose of enabling the second contribution condition for the then *unemployment benefit, sickness benefit and maternity allowance* to be fulfilled (see **24.1** above), a woman whose marriage had been terminated by the death of her husband or for any other reason was entitled, until 5 April 1987, to be credited with so many Class 1 contributions as were necessary to bring to the required level her EARNINGS FACTOR **(28)** for any tax year during the whole or part of which the marriage subsisted, provided that, during the tax year (if the marriage had by then taken place) before that in which the marriage ended, or during any subsequent tax year, she had derived an earnings factor of at least 25 times the weekly Lower Earnings Limit for the year in question from Class 1 or Class 2 contributions actually paid (see EARNINGS LIMITS AND THRESHOLDS **(33)**). [*Married Women etc. Regs, former Reg 2; Credits Regs, former Reg 10; Married Women and Widows Transitional Regs 1975, Reg 3; Credits Amendment Regs 1987, Reg 10*].

A marriage ended by divorce terminates on the date of the decree absolute. A voidable marriage which has been annulled is treated as if it was a valid marriage terminated by divorce at the date of the annulment. A woman who has obtained a decree absolute of presumption of death and dissolution of marriage is to be treated as a person whose marriage is terminated otherwise than on death, unless the date of her husband's death has been satisfactorily established. [former *Married Women etc. Regs, former Reg 10*].

Replace the first paragraph in 24.15 on pages 344 and 345 with the following:

Where a person ceases to be entitled either to a bereavement (formerly widow's) allowance or to a widowed parent's (formerly widowed mother's) allowance (other than by reason of remarriage or cohabitation with a man as his wife), they are to be treated as having satisfied the first contribution condition for contributions-based jobseeker's allowance, incapacity benefit or maternity allowance *and*, for the purpose of enabling the second contribution condition for any of those benefits to be fulfilled, they are to be credited with such Class 1 contributions as are necessary for every year up to and including that in which they ceased to be so entitled. The provisions extend to former civil partners with effect from 5 December 2005. [*Married Women etc. Regs, Reg 3(1)(a)(b)*, as amended by *Married Women and Widows Transitional Regs 1975, Reg 4 and Home Responsibilities Regs 1978, Reg 3(1); Credit Regs, Reg 8C inserted by Social Security (Benefits for Widows and Widowers) (Consequential Amendments) Regulations 2000, SI 2000/1483 and amended by Civil Partnership (Pensions, Social Security and Child Support) (Consequential, etc. Provisions) Order 2005, SI 2005/2877*].

Replace the last two paragraphs of 24.18 on page 347 with the following:

From 6 April 2003 a credit is also awarded as above for any week where a person is in receipt of Statutory Adoption Pay.

[*Credits Regs, Reg 9C*, as amended by *Credits Amendment Regs 2003, Reg 2(3)*].

Replace the last paragraph of 24.22 on page 349 with the following:

From April 2003, those receiving tax credits and whose Class 1 earnings do not reach the Lower Earnings Limit or who are self-employed and have claimed small earnings exception can usually receive a contribution credit for retirement pension, widowed parent's allowance and widow(er)s pension purposes. This applies to any claimant other than a married woman with a valid reduced rate election—see REDUCED LIABILITY ELECTIONS **(54)**, not just the disabled. However, in the case of those receiving a disability element of working tax credit (as specified in *Working Tax Credits (Entitlement and Maximum Rate) Regs 2002, Reg 20 (1)(b)(f)*) entitlement is to a credit for the purpose of all contributory (ie, including short-term) benefits. [*Credits Regs, Regs 7B, 7C* as amended by *Social Security (Working Tax Credit and Child Tax Credit) (Consequential Amendments) Regulations 2003, SI 2003/455, Sch 4, para 1*].

Insert the following paragraph after the first paragraph of 24.23 on page 349:

The *Social Security Pensions (Home Responsibilities) (Amendment) Regulations 2005, SI 2005/48*) provide that where the recipient of child benefit is switched during the first three months of a tax year, it shall be treated for the purpose of HRP as if made at the very start of that tax year. This change applies to switches made in 2004/05 onwards. The *Social Security Pensions (Home Responsibilities) Amendment Regulations 2008, SI 2008/498* go further and provide that HRP can be given to a claimant where their partner was paid child benefit for a whole tax year and during that year they were residing together, sharing care for a child under 16 and where the child benefit claimant does not themselves benefit from the HRP available due to having paid actual National Insurance contributions. This will only apply where the claimant reaches state pension age on or after 6 April 2008 (or in the case of bereavement benefit, the death is on or after 6 April 2008). Where a male partner has no NIC-able income and the female partner (who is the default claimant for child benefit) does, this is more flexible than the previous option to transfer which came into effect for 2004/05 onwards.

28   Earnings factors

Replace the statutory reference at the end of the first paragraph in 28.4 on page 365 with the following:

[*Earnings Factor Regs, Reg 2, Sch 1 para 2* as substituted by *Earnings Factor Amendment Regs 1991, Reg 3*].

Replace the statutory reference at the end of the first paragraph in 28.6 on page 367 with the following:

[*Earnings Factor Regs, Reg 2, Sch 1 para 4* as amended by *Earnings Factor Amendment Regs 1991, Reg 3*].

29   Earnings from employment: General

Replace the statutory reference at the end of 29.3 on page 375 with the following:

[*Social Security (Contributions) (Amendment No 8) Regs 2000, SI 2000/2207, Reg 4; Social Security (Contributions) (Amendment No 3) Regs 2001, SI 2001/596, Reg 7 and Social Security (Contributions) Regulations 2001, SI 2001/1004, Sch 3 Part X para 8; Social Security (Contributions) (Amendment No 2) Regs 2008, SI 2008/607, Reg 4; FA 2008, ss 46, 48 and 51*]. See also **16.1** CLASS 1A CONTRIBUTIONS: BENEFITS IN KIND.

Insert the following paragraph in 29.32 after the third paragraph on page 413;

On 13 June 2008, HM Revenue and Customs was successful in its appeal at the High Court (*Annabels (Berkeley Square) Ltd* [2007] EAT/0562/07). The Employment Tribunal had heard that sums held by a troncmaster belonged to the employees. But as things stand following the High Court decision such sums when distributed cannot form part of an employer's National Minimum Wage obligation. However, it is understood that Annabels was to further appeal. However, as many affected businesses now handle tips rather differently the success on the part of HM Revenue and Customs may be of limited value in its application to other cases currently. Perhaps for this reason, the Government subsequently announced in July 2008 that the National Minimum Wage legislation will be changed so that tips will not be able to be counted under any circumstances as part of an employee's NMW entitlement. This is expected to take effect sometime in 2009 and it is presumed that no changes will be required to the NIC legislation.

30   Earnings from employment: Expenses

Insert the following paragraph in the first paragraph of 30.12 on pages 435 and 436 prior to the last sentence in that paragraph:

Also in *HP Lewis v HMRC* [2008] Sp C 690 a Revenue officer (L) had worked for many years at HMRC offices within daily commuting distance of her home in Warwickshire. In 2000 she successfully applied for a post in London. She was allowed to work at the London office for two or three days each week, and from her home for two or three days each week. She claimed a deduction for the costs of travelling from Warwickshire to London. HMRC rejected the claim on the basis that this expenditure was 'ordinary commuting', which was not deductible by virtue of *ITEPA 2003, s 338*. The Special Commissioner upheld HMRC's ruling and dismissed L's appeal. See HMRC Booklets 480 (2008), Chapter 5 and 490, para 3.1.

31   Earnings from employment: Readily convertible assets, etc

Add the following sentence in place of the last sentence in the first paragraph in 31.2 on page 460 as follows:

From the 1 December 2008 where draft elections are presented for approval to HMRC and they include additional elements not required by the legislation nor essential for the implementation of the election then approval will not be given. Further guidance on NIC Elections can be found in

35   Enforcement

the Employment Related Securities Manual, ERSM 170750, 170760. See also IR Press Releases, 5 and 10 September 2003. See also CWG2 (2008), pages 95–97, Society of Share Scheme Practitioners November 1996, Budget Press Release and IR Press Release 189/00.

Insert the following paragraphs in place of the first two paragraphs on page 468 in 31.2:

The UK investment exchanges recognised under the *Financial Services and Markets Act 2000, s 287* as at 6 November 2008 are

EDX London Ltd

ICE Futures Europe

LIFFE Administration and Management (London International Financial Futures Exchange)

London Stock Exchange plc

PLUS Markets plc

SWX Europe Ltd

The London Metal Exchange Ltd

The overseas investment exchanges recognised under the *Financial Services and Markets Act 2000, s 287* by the Treasury as at 6 November 2008 are

Cantor Financial Futures Exchange (CFEE)

Chicago Board of Trade (CBOT)

EUREX Zurich

ICE futures US, Inc

National Association of Securities Dealers Automated Quotations (NASDAQ)

New York Mercantile Exchange (NYMEX Inc.)

NQLX LLC

Sydney Futures Exchange Ltd (SFE)

The Chicago Mercantile Exchange (CME)

The Swiss Stock Exchange (SWX)

US Futures Exchange LLC

35   Enforcement

Add the following sentence to the beginning of the last paragraph in 35.2 on page 513;

From 1 December 2007, *Taxes Management Act 1970, ss 20, 20B* and *20BB* are superseded since as part of HM Revenue and Customs the former Inland Revenue can now apply for search warrants under *Police and Criminal Evidence Act 1984*. [*Police and Criminal Evidence Act 1984 (Application and Customs) Order 2007, SI 2007/3175; Civil Evidence Act 1995; FA 2008, s 118, Sch 36 paras 65, 69*].

Substitute the following for the last two sentences in the first paragraph on page 519 in 35.10:

The date has not yet been determined. [*FA 2008, ss 127, 128, 129*].

40   Intermediaries

Replace the last paragraph on page 546 and the first paragraph on page 547 in 40.8 with the following:

In *Island Consultants Ltd v HMRC* [2007] STC SCD 482 Sp C 603 a company (C) provided the services of its controlling director (H) to a water company (S), through an employment agency, on a series of three-month contracts for a five-year computer project. HMRC issued a ruling that C was liable to pay Class 1 NICs in respect of H's income under the contract. The Special Commissioner upheld HMRC's ruling holding that under the 'hypothetical contract' required by the regulations, 'the factors predominantly point towards employment'. See also *MKM Computing Ltd v HMRC* [2008] STC SCD 403 Sp C 653; *Dragonfly Consulting Ltd v HMRC* [2008] STC SCD 430 Sp C 655; *First Word Software Ltd v HMRC* [2008] STC SCD 389 Sp C 652; *Datagate Services Ltd v HMRC* [2008] STC SCD 453 Sp C 656.

In 1998 *MKM Computing Ltd* agreed to provide E's (a controlling director) services to a company (P) which supplied contract workers. P agreed to provide E's services to another company (L). The Special Commissioner upheld HMRC's ruling and dismissed MKM's appeal, finding that the controlling director, E, was 'part and parcel of (L's) organisation' and holding that under the hypothetical contract required by the regulations, he would have been an employee. In *Dragonfly Consulting Ltd (D) Ch D [2008] EWHC 2113 (Ch)* was incorpo-rated to provide the services of its controlling director (B), who was a computer software engineer. In 2000 D agreed to provide B's services to an agency (DP) which in turn agreed to provide B's services to the Automobile Association. The Special Commissioner reviewed the evidence in detail, rejected this contention and dismissed the appeal. The Commissioner observed that B 'worked fairly regular hours during each engagement, ... worked on parts of a project which were allocated to him as part of the AA's teams, ... was integrated into the AA's business, ... and had a role similar to that of a professional employee'. The Chancery Division upheld the decision on appeal. Henderson J observed that there were 'slight, but potentially significant differences' between the wording of the statutory test laid down for NIC purposes and that laid down for income tax purposes. He observed that 'the NIC test requires the arrangements themselves to be embodied in a notional contract, and then asks whether the circumstances (undefined) are such that the worker would be regarded as employed; whereas the income tax test directs attention in the first instance to the services provided by the worker for the client, and then asks whether the circumstances ... are such that, if the services were provided under a contract directly between the client and the worker, the worker would be regarded as an employee of the client'. However, these differences did not affect the result in this case. On the evidence, the Commissioner was entitled to conclude that 'the nature and degree of the control by the AA under the hypothetical contract' pointed towards employment. *First Word Software Ltd* (F) was incorporated to provide the services of its controlling director (N), who was a computer consultant. In 2000 F agreed to provide N's services to a company (P) which provided software services to another company (R). HMRC's issued a ruling that the arrangements were within the *Social Security Contributions (Intermediaries) Regulations 2000, SI 2000 No 727*, and that F was liable to pay Class 1 NICs in respect of the payments which it made to N. F appealed, contending that if the services had been performed under a contract between N and R, N would not be regarded as an employee of R. The Special Commissioner reviewed the evidence in detail, accepted this contention and allowed F's appeal, finding that the relevant contract contained a right of substitution and 'the intention of the parties was that (N) was not obliged to perform the services personally'. On the evidence, N 'acted as a subcontractor, with responsibility for part only of a larger project, and not as an employee'. In *Datagate Services Ltd* (D) was incorporated to provide the services of its controlling director (B), who was a computer software consultant. In 2000 D agreed to provide B's services to a company (T) which provided software services to another company (M). HMRC issued a ruling that the arrangements were within *SI 2000 No 727*, and that D was liable to pay Class 1 NICs on the basis that the payments it received under the contract were emoluments which it paid to B. D appealed, contending that if the services had been performed under a contract between B and M, B would not be regarded as an employee of M. The Special Commissioner accepted this contention and allowed the appeal, finding that there was no 'ultimate right of control on the part of (M)' and that B was 'in business on his own account and was not a person working as an employee in someone else's business on the hypothetical requirements that the legislation requires'.

42   Late-Paid Contributions

Replace the last sentence in the fourth paragraph and the two subsequent paragraphs in 42.9 on page 594 with the following:

IR Press Releases 18/2001, 28 March 2001, 19 March 2002 and 55/2007, 8 August 2007, [*Finance Act 2001, replaced by Finance Act 2008, s 135(2)(13) and Social Security Contributions (Deferred Payments and Interest) Regulations, SI 2001/1818; Finance Act 2008, s 135*].

Following the summer 2007 floods in certain parts of the UK, any businesses that were affected will not have to pay interest on tax or NICs deferred as a result of any serious financial difficulties encountered. There is a HMRC number for assistance for those affected being 08453 000157 and it is available seven days a week, 8am to 8pm. [*Finance Act 2008, s 135*].

Under *Finance Act 2008, s 135(2)* that section applies in relation to 'any liability to the Commissioners arising under or by virtue of an enactment or a contract settlement' and so applies the foot and mouth and flood reliefs announced in summer 2007 and referred to in the previous two paragraphs without the need for separate NIC legislation.

43   Leaflets and Forms

Insert on pages 596 to 602 in place of the Leaflets section in 43.2 and 43.3.

43.2   Leaflets

HM Revenue and Customs, together with the DWP and its agencies, produce various leaflets, many of which are specifically aimed at employers (ie manuals, tables and fact cards) and these are listed below.

Leaflets regarding National Insurance Contributions are issued by HM Revenue and Customs (except for SA series leaflets, which are issued by the DWP). It should be noted that HM Revenue and Customs has withdrawn a number of NIC leaflets during 2005 and 2006. See **43.3** for application forms formerly contained in now withdrawn leaflets. Those leaflets that remain available can be obtained from

*local HM Revenue and Customs (NIC) offices

++ HMRC (Residency), NICO, Longbenton, NEWCASTLE UPON TYNE NE98 1ZZ or Department for Work and Pensions, Pensions and Overseas Benefits Directorate, Customer Service Unit, Room TC 109, NEWCASTLE UPON TYNE NE98 1BA.

** National Insurance Services for the Pensions Industry (NISPI), NICO, Longbenton, NEWCASTLE UPON TYNE NE98 1ZZ.

Employers Orderline (08457 646 646)

~~ only from the HM Revenue and Customs website

DWP only from http://www.dwp.gov.uk/lifeevent/benefits/social_security_agreements.asp

In addition, many of the leaflets for employers are on the Employer's CD-ROM (obtainable from the Employers Orderline 08457 646 646 and http://www.hmrc.gov.uk/employers/emp-form.htm)

National Insurance Leaflets

	Number	**Date**	**Name**
	AO 1	2008	The Adjudicator's Office for complaints about HM Revenue and Customs and the Valuation Office Agency
*	CA 04	Jan 04	Class 2 and Class 3 National Insurance contributions Direct Debit the easier way to pay
~~	CA 14	Jun 02	Termination of Contracted-out Employment Manual for Salary Related Pension Schemes and Salary Related Parts of Mixed Benefits Schemes
~~	CA 14A	Apr 02	Termination of Contracted-out Employment Manual for Money Purchase Pension Schemes and Money Purchase Parts of Mixed Benefits Schemes
~~	CA 14C	May 07	Contracted-out Guidance for Salary Related Pension Schemes and Salary Related Overseas Schemes
~~	CA 14D	May 07	Contracted-out Guidance for Money Purchase Pension Schemes and Money Purchase Overseas Schemes
~~	CA 14E	May 07	Contracted-out Guidance for Mixed Benefit Pension Schemes and Mixed Benefit Overseas Schemes
~~	CA 14F	Apr 03	Technical Guidance on Contracted-Out Decision Making and Appeals
~~	CA 15	Feb 05	Cessation of Contracted-out Pension Schemes Manual
~~	CA 16	Oct 08	Appropriate Personal Pension Scheme Manual – Procedural Guidance
~~	CA 16A	May 07	Appropriate Personal Pension Scheme Manual –Guidance for Scheme Managers
~~	CA 17	Apr 08	Employee's guide to minimum contributions
~~	CA 19	Apr 03	Using the Accrued GMP Liability Service
~~	CA 20	Mar 03	Using the Contracted-out Contributions/ Earnings Information Service
~~	CA 21	Jul 04	Using the National Insurance Number/Date of Birth Checking Service
~~	CA 22	Oct 02	Contracted-out Data Transactions using Magnetic Media
#	CA 33	Apr 07	Class 1A National Insurance contributions on Car and Fuel Benefits – A guide for employers
*	CA 37	Apr 08	Simplified Deductions Scheme for employers
#	CA 38	Apr 08	Not contracted-out Tables (Tables A, J)
#	CA 39	Apr 08	Contracted-out contributions for employers with Contracted-out Salary Related Schemes (Tables D, E, L)
#	CA 40	Apr 08	Employee only contributions tables for employers or employees authorised to pay their own contributions

43 Leaflets and Forms

#	CA 41	Apr 08	Not contracted-out Tables (Tables B and C)
~~	CA 42	Apr 08	Foreign-Going Mariner's and Deep Sea Fisherman's contributions for employers
#	CA 43	Apr 08	Contracted-out contributions and minimum payments for employers with contracted-out Money Purchase Schemes (Tables F, G, S)
#	CA 44	Dec 07	National Insurance for Company Directors (Employer Manual)
~~	CA 84	Oct 02	Stakeholder Pension Scheme Manual – Procedural Guidance
~~	CA 85		Contracted-out Stakeholder Pension Scheme Manual
*	CA 89	Sep 07	Payroll Cleansing. A free service offered by HMRC
**	CA 92	Feb 04	Services to Pensions Industry. An Information Guide
	CA 93	Jul 05	Shortfall in your NICs; National Insurance Contributions. To pay or not to pay?
~~	C/FS	Apr 07	Complaints and putting things right
*	COP 10	Apr 99	Inland Revenue: Information and advice
#	CWG 2	Dec 07	Employer Further Guide to PAYE and NICs
#	CWG 5	Dec 07	Class 1A National Insurance contributions on benefits in kind A guide for employers
*	CWL 2	Jun 03	National Insurance contributions for self-employed people. Class 2 and Class 4
#	E 10	Dec 07	Employer Help Book. Finishing the tax year up to 5 April 2008
#	E 11	Dec 07	Employer Help Book. Starting the tax year from 6 April 2008
#	E 12	Jul 08	Employer Help Book. PAYE and NICs rates and limits for 2008–09 (from September 2008)
#	E 13	Dec 07	Employer Help Book. Day-to-day payroll
#	E 13	Jun 08	Employer Help Book. Day-to-day payroll – Supplement to paper edition
	E 13	Jun 08	Employer Help Book. Day-to-day payroll (fully updated version on Employer CD-ROM only)
#	E 14	Dec 07	Employer Help Book. What to do if your employee is sick
#	E 15	Dec 07	Employer Help Book. Pay and time off work for parents. An employer guide to Statutory Maternity Pay and Leave and Statutory Paternity Pay and Leave
#	E 16	Dec 07	Pay and time off work for adoptive parents From 6 April 2008
~~	E 18	Apr 05	How you can help your employees with childcare
~~	E 24	2006	Tips, Gratuities, Service Charges and troncs. A guide to Income Tax, National Insurance contributions, National Minimum Wage issues, and VAT
~~	EC/FS1	Apr 08	Employers and contractors – reviewing your records

14

~	EC/FS2	Apr 08	Large employers and contractors – reviewing your records
~	EC/FS3	Apr 08	Compliance checks – what happens during and at the end of a check
~	EC/FS4	Apr 08	Compliance checks – types of penalty
~	EC/FS5	Apr 08	Employers and contractors compliance checks – your obligations
~	ES/FS1	Jun 08	Employed or self-employed for tax and National Insurance contributions
~	ES/FS2	Aug 08	Are your workers employed or self-employed for tax and National Insurance contributions
*	IR 115	Feb 05	Income tax, National Insurance contributions and childcare
*	IR 120	Sep 01	You and the Inland Revenue National Insurance Contributions Office
*	IR 121	Jul 06	Approaching retirement A guide to tax and National Insurance contributions
++	NI 38	Mar 08	Social Security abroad
	DWP SA 4	Oct 05	Social security agreement between the United Kingdom and Jersey and Guernsey
	DWP SA 8	Oct 05	Social security agreement between the United Kingdom and New Zealand
	DWP SA 14	Oct 03	Social security agreement between United Kingdom and Israel
	DWP SA 17	Oct 03	Social security agreement between United Kingdom and the Republics of the former Yugoslavia
	DWP SA 20	Oct 05	Social security agreement between the United Kingdom and Canada
	DWP SA 22	Oct 05	Social security agreement between the United Kingdom and Turkey
	DWP SA 23	Oct 03	Social security agreement between United Kingdom and Bermuda
	DWP SA 27	Oct 05	Social security agreement between United Kingdom and Jamaica
++	SA 29	Jan 06	Your social security insurance, benefits and healthcare rights in the European Community
	DWP SA 33	Oct 05	Social security agreement between the United Kingdom and United States of America
	DWP SA 38	Oct 03	Social security agreement between United Kingdom and Mauritius
	DWP SA 42	Oct 03	Social security agreement between the United Kingdom and Philippines
	DWP SA 43	Oct 03	Social security agreement between the United Kingdom and Barbados
*	SE 1	May 07	Are you thinking of working for yourself?

43   Leaflets and Forms

Other social security leaflets are available from local social security offices, except where indicated

* only available from Child Support Literature Line, Room 164E, DSS Longbenton, NEW-CASTLE UPON TYNE NE98 1YX (phone 08457 133133 fax 0191 2254572)

\+ only available from Department of Health, PO Box 777, LONDON SE1 6XH

\++ Pensions Guide, Freepost RLXH-JUEU-GZCH, NORTHAMPTON NN3 6DF (phone 08457 31 32 33, textphone 08456 040210)

** Phone 08701 555455; email: dh@prolog.uk.com

\# only available from Service Personnel & Veterans Agency Distribution Unit, Room 8102, Norcross, Thornton-Cleveleys FY5 3WP and http://www.veterans-uk.info/publications/leaflets.html

\~~ only from the DWP's website

	Number	Date	Name
	AAA5DCS	Jan 06	Attendance Allowance
	BR19L	Apr 08	State Pension forecast
	BRA5DWP	Apr 08	Social Security Benefit Rates
	CAA5DCS	Jan 06	Carer's Allowance
	CF 411	May 03	Home Responsibilities Protection
	CPF 2	Apr 06	A guide to combined pension forecasts
*	CSA 2001	Dec 05	Child Support for parents who live apart
*	CSA 2002	May 01	Changes in child maintenance. Advice to Employers
*	CSL 301	Apr 07	What is child maintenance and how does it affect me?
*	CSL 302	Apr 07	How do I get child maintenance if I'm on benefits?
*	CSL 303	Aug 07	How is child maintenance worked out?
*	CSL 304	Apr 07	What happens if someone denies they are the parent of a child?
*	CSL 305	Apr 07	How do I pay child maintenance?
*	CSL 306	Apr 07	What action can the Child Support Agency take if parents don't pay?
*	CSL 307	Apr 07	How can I appeal against a child maintenance decision?
*	CSL 308	Apr 07	How do I complain about the service I get from the Child Support Agency?
*	CSL 309	Apr 07	How do I apply for child maintenance? For children living in Scotland
*	CSL 310	Apr 07	Why is the Child Support Agency changing my child maintenance and how will it be different?
*	CSL 311	Apr 07	How does the Child Support Agency use and store information?
*	CSL 312	Dec 05	Child Support: a technical guide
*	CSL 313	Apr 07	What is my role in helping my employees pay child maintenance?

16

*	CSL 314	Apr 07	How will I receive child maintenance?
	CTA5DWP	May 06	Help with your Council Tax
	D 49	Apr 06	What to do after a death in England and Wales
~	DB 1	Apr 08	A guide to Industrial Injuries Schemes Benefits
	DCRA5JP	May 06	Just for the record – help and advice for people with a criminal record
	DHC1JP	Jun 05	A guide for disabled people, those with health conditions and carers
	DLAA5DCS	Jan 06	Disability Living Allowance
	DLACA5DCS	Jan 06	Disability Living Allowance for children
	DWP1001	Feb 08	Incapacity Benefit
	DWP1002	May 08	Jobseekers Allowance
	DWP1003	Mar 08	Income Support
	DWP1004	May 08	Industrial Injuries Disablement Benefit
	DWP1006	May 08	National Insurance
	DWP1007	Feb 08	Social Fund
	DWP1008	Feb 08	Workpath
	DWP1009	Feb 08	New Deal 50 plus
	DWP1010	Feb 08	New Deal 25 plus
	DWP1011	Mar 08	New Deal for Disabled People
	DWP1012	Feb 08	New Deal for Young People
	DWP1013	Mar 08	New Deal for Musicians
	DWP1014	Feb 08	Progress2work
	DWP1016	Feb 08	Help with job interviews
	DWP1017	Mar 08	Finding a job
	DWP1018	Feb 08	Being a mentor
	DWP1019	May 08	Permitted Work
	DWP1020	Feb 08	Statutory Sick Pay
	DWP1021	Mar 08	The Disability Symbol and the Disability Discrimination Act
	DWP1022	Feb 08	Share Fisherman
	DWP1023	Jun 08	Volunteering while receiving benefits
	DWP1024	Mar 08	Our service standards
	DWP1025	May 08	Tell us what you think
	DWP1026	Jan 08	Help if you are ill or disabled
	DWP1029	May 08	Going into hospital
	ETBA5JP	May 06	How education and training affects your Jobseeker's Allowance

43 Leaflets and Forms

	EZA5JP	May 06	Employment Zones
	GIHA5DWP	Jun 06	Going into hospital
	GL 22	Jun 08	Tell us how to improve our service
	GL 24DWP	Jun 08	If you think our decision is wrong
	GL 27	Aug 05	Compensation and social security benefits
~~	HB 5	Jan 06	A guide to Non-contributory Benefits for Disabled People & their Carers
	HBA5DWP	May 06	Help with your rent
	HHBA5JP	Mar 06	Help with getting benefits for people with a disability or health condition
+	HC 11	Aug 03	Are you entitled to help with health costs?
	HC 11QG	May 06	Help with Health Costs Quick Guide
+	HC 11(TC)	Apr 03	New Tax Credits Help With NHS Costs
+	HC 12	Sep 03	NHS charges and optical voucher values
~~	IS 20	Apr 05	A guide to Income Support
	JSA60A5JP	May 06	JSA over 60 or nearing 60
	JSASTWA5JP	Dec 05	If you are working short time or are laid off
#	Leaflet 1	Apr 07	Notes about the War Disablement Pension and War Widows or Widowers Pension
#	Leaflet 2	Apr 07	Notes for people getting a War Pension living in the United Kingdom
#	Leaflet 3	Apr 07	Notes for people getting a War Pension living overseas
#	Leaflet 4	Apr 07	Notes about rejected claims for War Disablement and War Widows or Widowers pensions living in the United Kingdom
#	Leaflet 5	Apr 07	Notes about rejected claims for War Disablement and War Widows or Widowers pensions living overseas
#	Leaflet 6	Apr 07	Notes for War Pensioners and War Widows or Widower pensioners going abroad
#	Leaflet 7	Apr 07	Notes for Ex-Far East and Korean Prisoners of War
#	Leaflet 9	Apr 08	Rates of War Pensions and allowances 2008–2009
#	Leaflet 10	Apr 07	Notes about War Pension claims for deafness
#	Leaflet 11	Apr 08	How we decide who receives a War Disablement Pension
#	Leaflet 12	Apr 03	Ex-Gratia payment for British troops who were held prisoner by the Japanese during World War Two
#	Leaflet 13	Oct 03	Complaints Listening Learning Acting Improving
#	Leaflet 14	Jun 04	A Guide To Direct Payment
	LP1JP	Nov 05	A guide for lone parents
	LP 15	Aug 03	New deal Lone parents
	MORTA5DWP	May 06	Help with your mortgage

~	NI 17A	Apr 08	A guide to Maternity Benefits
~	NI 260	Apr 04	A guide to Dispute, Supersession and Appeal
~	NP 45	Apr 05	A guide to Bereavement Benefits
	NP 46	Jun 08	A guide to State Pensions
++	OVER50	Apr 06	Are you over 50? A practical guide to advice, support and services across government
	OW1JP	Nov 05	A guide for people who are out of work
	PC1L	Oct 08	Pension Credit: Do I qualify and how much could I get?
	PG1	Oct 07	Pensioners' guide
++	PM 2	Feb 08	State pensions. Your guide
++	PM 7	Jan 08	Contracted-out pensions. Your guide
	PME 1	Nov 05	Stakeholder pensions. A guide for employers
	PSCUST1	Jun 07	The Pension Service Customer Charter
	PTB 1	Sep 06	Pensions: the basics. A guide from the Government
	PWA5JP	Apr 06	Permitted Work
++	QG 1	Feb 06	A quick guide to pensions
	QGJSAA5JP	Jun 06	Jobseekers allowance
	REFA5JP	May 06	Help for refugees
~	RR 2	Dec 05	A guide to Housing Benefit and Council Tax Benefit
~	SB 16	Apr 08	A guide to The Social Fund
	SDA5DWP	Jun 06	Separated, Divorced or Civil Partnership dissolved?
	SEA5JP	Feb 07	Ever thought of working for yourself?
	SERPSL 1	Dec 07	Inheritance of SERPS. Important information for married people
	SFA5JP	Jan 06	Share Fishermen
++	SPD 1	Apr 06	Your State Pension Choice – Pension now or extra pension later. A guide to State Pension Deferral
++	SPD 2	Sep 07	Deferring your State Pension
**	T 7.1	May 06	Health advice for Travellers
	TIOSA5JP	Sep 06	Tap into our services
	VACDPA5DCS	Jan 06	Vaccine Damage Payments
	VFWA5JP	May 06	Volunteering while unemployed helps others and can help you
	WFPL 1	Aug 08	Your guide to Winter Fuel Payments and Cold Weather Payments 2008/09
	WIDA5DWP	Apr 06	If you are widowed or your civil partner dies
#	WPA GV1	Mar 03	Claims for War Pensions Notes for Gulf Veterans
#	WPWS-1		War Pensioners' Welfare Service Serving Those Who Served

43   Leaflets and Forms

～	Z 1	Aug 05	Recovery of benefits and NHS charges. Procedures for liaison with the Compensation Recovery
～	Z 2	Aug 05	Recovery of benefits. Appeal Guide

43.3   Application forms

A number of leaflets that HM Revenue and Customs has completely withdrawn in 2005 and 2006 (ie it is not simply the case that they are only available on the internet) contained important application/claim forms. These can now be downloaded from http://www.hmrc.gov.uk/leaflets/obsolete.htm and are as follows

Former leaflet	Form	Form title
CA 02	CF 10	Application for exception for liability for Class 2 contributions (small earnings exception)
CA 08	CA 5603	To pay voluntary National Insurance contributions
CA 09	CF 9A	National Insurance contributions for widows or widowers
CA 13	CF 9	Married woman application for a certificate of election or to change to full liability
CA 72	CA 72A	Application for deferment of payment of Class 1 contributions
CA 72	CA 72B	Application for deferment of payment of Class 2 and Class 4 contributions

Other forms (though some are duplicated from the above list) can be downloaded from http://www.hmrc.gov.uk/nic/forms.htm as follows

Form	Form title
CA 1586	National Insurance Services to Pension Industry Forms – list and order form
CA 5601	Application to pay Class 2 National Insurance contributions by Direct Debit
CA 5603	To pay voluntary National Insurance contributions
CA 6855	Employers application for National Insurance Number Trace
CA 72A	Application for deferment of payment of Class 1 contributions
CA 72B	Application for deferment of payment of Class 2 and Class 4 contributions
CA 82	If you think our decision is wrong
CF 9	Married woman application for a certificate of election or to change to full liability
CF 9A	National Insurance contributions for widows or widowers
CF 351N	Application to pay National Insurance contributions by Direct Debit
CF 411	Home Responsibilities Protection (HRP) – application form
CF 411 Notes	Home Responsibilities Protection (HRP) – notes
RD1299a	Your National Insurance Contributions

CA 72A and CA 72B forms in relation to deferment applications (including some forms for older years) are obtainable from http://www.hmrc.gov.uk/individuals/fgcat-deferment.shtml

Forms in connection with international matters can be downloaded from http://www.hmrc.gov.uk/cnr/osc.htm#6 as follows

Form	Form title
CA 3638	National Insurance Contributions – How you can get a Retirement Pension Forecast
CA 3821	National Insurance Contributions – For employers whose employees are going to work in a European Economic Area (EEA)/Reciprocal Agreement Country
CA 3822	National Insurance Contributions – Application for a certificate of continuing UK liability, including form E101 – when employees are going to work abroad
CA 3837	National Insurance Contributions – Application for form E101 when a self-employed person goes to work in the European Economic Area (EEA)
CA 8421	Application for form E101 when an employee is employed in two or more countries of the EEA
CA 8450	Application for certificate of continuing liability for groups of performers and crew (employed persons)
CA 8451	Application for certificate of continuing liability for groups of performers and crew (self-employed persons)
CA 8454	Application for certificate E106 or E109

46 Ministers of Religion

Add the following paragraph to the end of the second paragraph in 46.1 on page 617:

Also an employment tribunal has ruled that a church organist is an employee of the Church of England and will have full employment rights. In a recent landmark ruling concerning an organist and choirmaster who was dismissed and then brought a claim for unfair dismissal the church authorities had said he was not an employee. During the tribunal, church authorities argued the organist was self-employed because he agreed to be paid gross without any deduction under the PAYE system. The judge said that the tax treatment of an individual is irrelevant in determining employment status. The ruling means that, after a years service, organists in the Church of England may now bring a claim for unfair dismissal against the vicar and the parochial church council if sacked without good reason.

50 Oil-Rig Workers, Divers, etc

Add the following sentence at the end of the second paragraph of 50.3 on page 639:

In *JAL Mason v HMRC* from 1983 to 1998 an electrician (M) had been employed on drilling rigs in the North Sea. His employers reduced his monthly salary by withholding a small 'retainer', which they then paid two weeks later. For NIC purposes, his employers treated him as having two-weekly pay periods rather than four-weekly pay periods. The consequences were that the employers avoided paying NIC on the 'retainer' payments, on the basis that these payments fell below the lower limit for NICs for the notional fortnightly period, and that they paid less NIC than they would otherwise have done in respect of the balancing payments, on the basis that much of the payment exceeded the upper limit for NICs for the notional fort-nightly period. The effect of the way in which his employers had paid him was that he received

. a lower state pension than he would have done if his employers had paid him monthly. The Commissioner observed that it seemed 'strange that officials would have been ignorantly oblivious to what was happening, and to the unrealistic effect of the practice'. He expressed the view that M had 'a genuine and significant grievance'. See *JAL Mason v HMRC* [2008] Sp C 712.

51   Overseas Matters

Insert the following paragraph after the third paragraph in 51.14 on page 667:

The full text of *ACR 16* is as follows –

'RECOMMENDATION No 16 of 12 December 1984 concerning the conclusion of agreements pursuant to Article 17 of Council Regulation (EEC) No 1408/71(85/C 273/03)

THE ADMINISTRATIVE COMMISSION OF THE EUROPEAN COMMUNITIES ON SOCIAL SECURITY FOR MIGRANT WORKERS, Having regard to the opinion of the Advisory Committee on Social Security for Migrant Workers, adopted at its 15th meeting on 11 April 1984, Whereas Article 17 of Regulation (EEC) No 1408/71 lays down that two or more Member States, the competent authorities of those States or the bodies designated by those authorities may, by common agreement, provide for exceptions to the provisions of the aforementioned Regulation concerning the determination of the legislation applicable in the interests of certain categories of employed or self-employed persons, or of certain such persons; Whereas certain employed persons, by virtue of their special knowledge and skills or because of specific objectives set by the undertaking or organization with which they are employed, are posted abroad to the territory of a Member State other than the one in which they are normally employed in the interests of, in the name of, or on behalf of that undertaking or organization for a period of more than 12 months; Whereas it is recommended that in the interests of these employed persons, they should be allowed to choose between being subject to the legislation of the Member State of employment or remaining subject to the legislation of the Member State where they are normally employed for the duration of the posting abroad, RECOMMENDS to the competent authorities of the Member States that they conclude, or have concluded by the bodies designated by these competent authorities, agreements pursuant to Article 17 of Regulation (EEC) No 1408/71 applicable to employed persons who, by virtue of their special knowledge and skills or because of specific objectives set by the undertaking or organization with which they are employed are posted abroad to a Member State other than the one in which they are normally employed in the interests of, in the name of, or on behalf of that undertaking or organization for a period exceeding 12 months. These agreements should lay down that these employed persons remain subject to the legislation of the sending State for the full duration of their assignment provided that the workers concerned agree to this condition. J. DOWNEY Chairman of the Administrative Commission.'

Replace the section in 51.23 on page 678 with the following:

51.23   Multilateral agreements

Apart from the EC Treaty itself, the most important multilateral treaties affecting contribution law are the EC Co-operation Agreements entered into between the EC and Switzerland, Algeria, Morocco and Tunisia, ie Maghreb. That with Switzerland came into effect on 1 June 2002. When the remaining treaties are fully implemented, the EC regulations on contribution law will extend to the other states mentioned also. There are also proposals for similar agreements in the cases of Croatia, former Yugoslav Republic of Macedonia and Israel.

53 Rates and Limits

Replace the section 53.14 on pages 697 and 698 with the following:

53.14 Interest

Interest is due on overdue contributions (except Class 2 and Class 3) from 19 April 1993. Interest on overpayments of Class 1 contributions arises from the same date but on repayments of Class 4 contributions only from 6 April 1995. See http://www.hmrc.gov.uk/rates/interest.htm

From	Overdue contributions	Overpaid contributions
	%	%
6 December 2008	5.5	1.50
6 November 2008	6.5	2.25
6 January 2008	7.5	3.00
6 August 2007	8.5	4.00
6 September 2006	7.5	3.00
6 September 2005	6.5	2.25
6 September 2004	7.5	3.00
6 December 2003	6.5	2.25
6 August 2003	5.5	1.50
6 November 2001	6.5	2.25
6 May 2001	7.5	3.00
6 February 2000	8.5	4.00
6 March 1999	7.5	3.00
6 January 1999	8.5	4.00
6 August 1997	9.5	4.75
31 January 1997	8.5	4.00
6 February 1996	6.25	6.25
6 March 1995	7.0	7.00
6 October 1994	6.25	6.25
6 January 1994	5.5	5.50
6 March 1993	6.25	6.25

57 Subpostmasters

Replace the last sentence of 57.1 on page 721 with the following:

In all there are three categories of Post Office, numbering in all just under 14,000 offices, reducing to 12,250 by 2009. The first is Crown Post Offices, of which there were 393 as at 30

57   Subpostmasters

March 2008. The second is main post offices of which there are three types (see below). The third is the true sub-Post Office (also known as agency post offices) – these form the vast majority of the 14,000 offices and of these the majority are governed by a 'Subpostmasters Contract (1994 version) (R6)'. The second category referred to above comprises franchised main post offices, independent offices within large stores, and modified sub-post offices. Modified sub-post offices are Crown Post Offices which have been put out to contract. Modified subpostmasters are employees of the Post Office.

PRE-BUDGET REPORT PRESS RELEASES RELATING TO NICs

INCOME TAX RATES, ALLOWANCES AND LIMITS AND NATIONAL INSURANCE CONTRIBUTIONS RATES AND THRESHOLDS

Who is likely to be affected?

1. All individual income tax payers, employers, employees, the self employed and trustees.

General description of the measure

2. This measure sets the income tax personal allowances and related amounts and the rates and rates limits for the 2009-10 tax year, as well as making a number of other changes.

3. For 2009-10 the Upper Earnings Limit (UEL) for primary Class 1 National Insurance Contributions (NICs) will be aligned with the level at which people start to pay higher rate income tax.

4. From 2010-11 the basic personal allowance for income tax will be reduced in two stages for those with gross incomes above £100,000 and £140,000.

5. From 2011-12 there will be higher rates of tax for income above £150,000.

6. From 2011-12 there will be increases to the dividend trust rate and the trust rate of tax.

7. From 2011-12 the NICs primary threshold will be broadly aligned with the income tax basic personal allowance.

8. From 2011-12 the main rate of Class 1 and Class 4 NICs will be increased by 0.5 per cent to 11.5 per cent and 8.5 per cent respectively.

9. From 2011-12 the Class 1 employer rate of NICs will be increased by 0.5 per cent to 13.3 per cent. The increased rate will also apply to Class 1A and Class 1B contributions.

10. From 2011-12 the additional rate of Class 1 and 4 NICs will be increased by 0.5 per cent to 1.5 per cent.

Operative date

2009-10

11. The amounts of income tax personal allowances and related amounts and the rates and rate bands will have effect on and after 6 April 2009.

12. The UEL for Class 1 NICs will be aligned with the level at which people start to pay higher rate income tax on and after 6 April 2009.

2010-11

13. There will be two separate income limits for the basic personal allowance. The personal allowance will be reduced for individuals with gross incomes before personal allowances above £100,000 and £140,000 on and after 6 April 2010.

2011-12

14. A new 45 per cent rate of income tax will apply to taxable non-savings and savings income above £150,000 on and after 6 April 2011.

15. A new 37.5 per cent rate of tax will apply to taxable dividend income above £150,000 on and after 6 April 2011.

16. The dividend trust rate and the trust rate of tax will be increased to 37.5 per cent and 45 per cent respectively from 6 April 2011.

17. The changes to the NICs primary threshold, the main rates of Class 1, Class 4, Class 1 employer rate, Class 1A, Class 1B and the additional rates of Class 1 and Class 4 NICs will have effect on and after 6 April 2011.

Current law and proposed revisions

18. For 2009-10, the main rates of income tax will be the 20 per cent basic rate and the 40 per cent higher rate.

19. The basic personal allowance for 2008-09 was increased above indexation from £5,225 to £6,035. For 2009-10 the allowance will be increased by £130 above indexation from £6,035 to £6,475.

20. The basic rate limit for 2009-10 will be increased by £800 above indexation from £34,800 to £37,400.

21. For 2009-10, all other personal allowances, the income limit for age-related allowances, the minimum amount of married couple's allowance and the starting rate limit for savings income will be increased by indexation, as set out in the table below:

Personal allowances and rate limits for 2009-10

	2008-09	2009-10
Basic personal allowance	£6,035	£6,475
Personal allowance for those aged 65 to 74	£9,030	£9,490
Personal allowance for those aged 75 and over	£9,180	£9,640
Blind person's allowance	£1,800	£1,890
Married couple's allowance	£6,625	£6,965
Income limit for age-related allowances	£21,800	£22,900
Minimum amount of married couple's allowance	£2,540	£2,670
Basic rate limit	£34,800	£37,400
Starting rate limit for savings income	£2,320	£2,440

22. The basic personal allowance provides an amount of tax free income. All individuals entitled to the basic personal allowance receive the same amount. From 2010-11, the basic personal allowance will be subject to income limits of £100,000 and £140,000. Where an individual's gross income before personal allowances and any other deductions detailed in paragraph 25 is below or equal to the £100,000 income limit, they will continue to be entitled to the full amount of the basic personal allowance.

23. If an individual's gross income is above the income limit of £100,000, the amount of their allowance will be reduced by £1 for every £2 above the income limit up to a maximum of one half of the basic personal allowance. Because the last digit of the basic personal allowance is a five, where the full reduction applies the remaining amount of the basic personal allowance will be rounded up.

24. If an individual's gross income is above a second income limit of £140,000, the amount of their allowance will be further reduced by £1 for every £2 above the income limit up to a maximum of the full amount of the basic personal allowance.

25. For the purposes of the income-related reductions to the personal allowance, gross income comprises total income (as defined in section 23 of the Income Tax Act 2007) after the deduction of trading losses.

26. From April 2011 taxable non-savings and savings income above £150,000 will be liable to income tax at 45 per cent.

27. From 2011-12, there will be three rates of tax for dividends. Dividends otherwise taxable at the basic rate will continue to be taxable at the 10 per cent dividend ordinary rate and dividends otherwise taxable at the higher rate will continue to be taxable at the 32.5 per cent dividend upper rate. Dividends otherwise taxable at the new 45 per cent rate will be liable to income tax at a new rate of 37.5 per cent.

28. From 2011-12 the dividend trust rate will be increased from 32.5 per cent to 37.5 per cent and the trust rate of tax will be increased from 40 per cent to 45 per cent.

29. The point at which people start to pay higher rate tax (sometimes called the "higher rate threshold") is the total of the basic personal allowance and the basic rate limit. For 2009-10 this amount is £43,875. For 2008-09 the UEL for primary Class 1 NICs is £770 per week (£40,040 for the year). For 2009-10 the UEL will be increased to £844 per week with an annual equivalent of £43,875 for the year so that with necessary rounding to whole pounds, the UEL (which is a weekly figure) is aligned with the total of the basic personal allowance and the basic rate limit.

30. The changes to the main and additional rates of Class 1 and 4 NICs in 2011-12 will require a National Insurance Contributions Bill before they can be implemented.

Further advice

31. If you have any questions about the changes to income tax, please contact Paul Thomas on 020 7147 2479 (email: paul.thomas@hmrc.gsi.gov.uk). If you have any questions about the changes to National Insurance Contributions, please contact Kevin Rice on 020 7147 2514 (email: kevin.rice@hmrc.gsi.gov.uk). Information about Pre-Budget Report measures is available on the HM Revenue & Customs website at www.hmrc.gov.uk

VALUE ADDED TAX, INCOME TAX ALLOWANCES, NATIONAL INSURANCE CONTRIBUTIONS, CHILD AND WORKING TAX CREDIT RATES 2009-10 AND OTHER RATES

2009-10 rates and allowances for Value Added Tax, Income Tax, National Insurance Contributions, the Working and Child Tax Credits and Child Benefit/Guardian's Allowance are set out below.

Value Added Tax (VAT)

	Current rate	On and after 1 Dec 2008	On and after 1 Jan 2010
Standard rate	17.5%	15%	17.5%

Income tax personal and age-related allowances

£ per year (unless stated)	2008-09	Change	2009-10
Personal allowance (age under 65)	£6,035	+£440	£6,475
Personal allowance (age 65-74)	£9,030	+£460	£9,490
Personal allowance (age 75 and over)	£9,180	+£460	£9,640
Married couple's allowance* (aged less than 75 and born before 6th April 1935)	£6,535	+£330	£6,865

Pre-Budget Report Press Releases

Income tax personal and age-related allowances (continued)

£ per year (unless stated)	2008-09	Change	2009-10
Married couple's allowance* (age 75 and over)	£6,625	+£340	£6,965
Married couple's allowance* - minimum amount	£2,540	+£130	£2,670
Income limit for age-related allowances	£21,800	+£1,100	£22,900
Blind person's allowance	£1,800	+£90	£1,890
Pension schemes allowances			
Annual Allowance	£235,000	+£10,000	£245,000
Lifetime Allowance	£1,650,000	+£100,000	£1,750,000

*Married couple's allowance is given at the rate of 10 per cent.

Income tax: taxable bands

£ per year (unless stated)	2008-09	Change	2009-10
Starting savings rate 10%*	£0-£2,320	+£120	£0-2,440
Basic rate: 20%*	£0-34,800	+£2,600	£0-37,400
Higher rate: 40%*	Over £34,800	+£2,600	Over £37,400

*There is a 10p starting rate for savings only. If an individual's non savings taxable income exceeds the starting rate limit, the 10p starting rate for savings will not be available for savings income.

National Insurance contributions

£ per week (unless stated)	2008-09	Change	2009-10
Lower earnings limit, primary Class 1	£90	+£5	£95
Upper earnings limit, primary Class 1	£770	+£74	£844
Upper accruals point	n/a	n/a	£770
Primary threshold	£105	+£5	£110
Secondary threshold	£105	+£5	£110
Employees' primary Class 1 rate between primary threshold and upper earnings limit	11%	-	11%
Employees' primary Class 1 rate above upper earnings limit	1%	-	1%
Employees' contracted-out rebate - salary-related schemes	1.6%	-	1.6%
Employees' contracted-out rebate - money-purchase schemes	1.6%	-	1.6%
Married women's reduced rate between primary threshold and upper earnings limit	4.85%	-	4.85%
Married women's rate above upper earnings limit	1%	-	1%
Employers' secondary Class 1 rate above secondary threshold	12.8%	-	12.8%
Employers' contracted-out rebate, salary-related schemes	3.7%	-	3.7%

National Insurance contributions (continued)

£ per week (unless stated)	2008-09	Change	2009-10
Employers' contracted-out rebate, money-purchase schemes	1.4%	-	1.4%
Class 2 rate (per week)	£2.30	+£0.10	£2.40
Class 2 small earnings exception	£4,825 per year	+£250	£5,075 per year
Special Class 2 rate for share fishermen (per week)	£2.95	+0.10	£3.05
Special Class 2 rate for volunteer development workers	£4.50	+£0.25	£4.75
Class 3 rate (per week)	£8.10	+£3.95	£12.05
Class 4 lower profits limit	£5,435 per year	+£280	£5,715 per year
Class 4 upper profits limit	£40,040 per year	+£3,835	£43,875 per year
Class 4 rate between lower profits limit and upper profits limit	8%	-	8%
Class 4 rate above upper profits limit	1%	-	1%

Working and Child Tax Credits rates

Working Tax Credit

£ per year (unless stated)	2008-09	Change	2009-10
Basic element	£1,800	+£90	£1,890
Couple and lone parent element	£1,770	+£90	£1,860
30 hour element	£735	+£40	£775
Disabled worker element	£2,405	+£125	£2,530
Severe disability element	£1,020	+£55	£1,75
50+ Return to work payment (16-29 hours)	£1,235	+£65	£1,300
50+ Return to work payment (30+ hours)	£1,840	+£95	£1,935

Childcare element of the Working Tax Credit

£ per year (unless stated)	2008-09	Change	2009-10
Maximum eligible cost for one child	£175 per week	-	£175 per week
Maximum eligible cost for two or more children	£300 pw	-	£300 pw
Percentage of eligible costs covered	80%	-	80%

Pre-Budget Report Press Releases

Child Tax Credit

£ per year (unless stated)	2008-09	Change	2009-10
Family element	£545	-	£545
Family element, baby addition	£545	-	£545
Child element	£2,085	+£150	£2,235
Disabled child element	£2,540	+£130	£2,670
Severely disabled child element	£1,020	+£55	£1,075

Income thresholds and withdrawal rates

£ per year (unless stated)	2008-09	Change	2009-10
First income threshold	£6,420	-	£6,420
First withdrawal rate (per cent)	39%	-	39%
Second income threshold	£50,000	-	£50,000
Second withdrawal rate (per cent)	6.67%	-	6.67%
First threshold for those entitled to Child Tax Credit only	£15,575	+£465	£16,040
Income disregard	£25,000	-	£25,000

Child Benefit/Guardian's Allowance Rates

£ per week (unless stated)	2008-09	Change	2009-10
Eldest/Only Child	£18.80	+£1.20	£20.00
Other Children	£12.55	+£0.65	£13.20
Guardian's Allowance	£13.45	+£0.65	£14.10

National insurance contributions

The starting point for employers', employees' and self-employed NICs in 2009-10 will increase in line with inflation to £110 per week. NICs are not paid on earnings or profits below this amount. The upper earnings and profits limits for NICs will increase from £770 to £844 per week. For the self-employed, the rate of Class 2 contributions will increase to £2.40 per week.

The weekly rate of voluntary Class 3 contributions for the 2009/10 tax year will be £12.05 per week. This rate supports an amendment to the Pensions Bill, tabled by DWP Ministers on 29 October 2008, that relaxes the time limits for the payment of voluntary NICs by individuals approaching state pension age. The amendment allows individuals with 20 qualifying years on their record (which may include any complete year of Home Responsibilities Protection who reach State Pension age between 6 April 2008 and 5 April 2015 to pay an additional six years of voluntary Class 3 contributions for any missing years since 1975/76. As announced during the Bill debate, this rate is designed to make the amendment cost neutral overall. The number of qualifying years required to receive a full State Pension falls from 44 for a man and 39 for a woman to 30 for both men and women from 6 April 2010. This significantly increases the value of voluntary Class 3 contributions to those who buy them. The actuarial value of Class 3 contributions is around £45 per week.

Employers' and employees' contributions

In line with the Social Security Contributions and Benefits Act 1992, the lower earnings limit for employees' Class 1 contributions is to be raised to £95 a week. It is set at the level of the basic state pension for a single person from April 2009, rounded down to the nearest pound. This is the lowest level of weekly earnings that can count towards entitlement to contributory benefits.

The primary and secondary thresholds for Class 1 contributions will increase in line with inflation to £110 a week. Employees and employers will pay no Class 1 contributions on earnings below this level.

The upper earnings limit for employees' Class 1 contributions will be raised to £844 a week, aligning it with the weekly equivalent of the higher rate threshold, the level at which higher rate tax starts to be paid.

The standard main rate of employees' Class 1 contributions below the upper earnings limit will continue to be 11 per cent, and above the limit the rate will continue to be 1 per cent.

The standard rate of employers' Class 1 contributions will continue to be 12.8 per cent.

The self-employed

The flat rate of Class 2 contributions will increase to £2.40 a week. Those with earnings below the annual small earnings exception can apply to be exempted from paying Class 2 contributions; this limit will be raised to £5,075.

The annual lower profits limit for Class 4 contributions will increase in line with inflation to £5,715.

The upper profits limit for Class 4 contributions will be raised to £43,875, to align it with the level at which higher rate tax begins to be paid.

The self-employed will pay Class 4 contributions on all their profits above the lower profits limit. The rate of Class 4 contributions will continue to be 8 per cent on profits below the upper profits limit, and 1 per cent on profits above that limit.